Self-Esteem

Unleash Your Latent Abilities By Engaging In Personal Development And Cultivating Self-Assurance

(A Practical Manual For Overcoming Self Limiting Beliefs And Controlling Your Emotions)

Folkert de Ruijter

TABLE OF CONTENT

Introduction 1

Advice For Talking With Anyone About Anything . 31

Acquiring The Ability To Receive Praise 38

Establishing And Reaching Goals 64

The Empirical Evidence For Self-Compassion 108

Effects On Personality And Social Bonds 125

Emotional Intelligence 139

Introduction

All of us who are parents want to raise kids who have faith in their future. But for decades, parenting gurus had it all wrong, believing that complimenting kids on things like "smart" and "good job" would make them feel more confident and good about themselves. A decade's worth of rigorous research indicates that this may be detrimental, even deadly, to youngsters. According to other research, self-esteem originates from the "turn inside out" process rather than from the language used to interact with kids.

Does praising a child as a "good boy" or a "smart boy" have no impact on the child's confidence or self-esteem if it doesn't work? Fortunately, the most recent research on parenting demonstrates that raising children's self-esteem and confidence can help them succeed in the long run. This book's goal is to provide you with the tools you need to help your kids grow in confidence and self-worth so they can meet the difficulties of a stronger, smarter, and better life.

Self-worth and self-assurance are intimately linked, and both are essential for managing life's obstacles and unavoidable ups and downs. Self-esteem is our emotional assessment of our own ideals, first and foremost. Instead, it's a matrix through which we act, think, feel, and reflect, influencing how we relate to one another and the outside world.

Since self-esteem is mainly a mirror of our inner selves, it is a rather abstract notion. In contrast, self-confidence is linked to our behavior and how we interact with the outside world. One can acquire and grow confidence. With practice and repetition, we can improve at anything. But just having a high degree of confidence might not be sufficient to bring prosperity and happiness to an individual since it is insufficient to have confidence in one area while lacking it in another. It's true that people can have high or low self-esteem, but low self-esteem can be especially harmful because self-assured people are more likely to take chances and take on new challenges.

The secret to success in all facets of life, both emotionally and professionally, is having a high sense of self-worth. They have a significant impact on our self-perception, and whether those perceptions are favorable or unfavorable, they frequently show up in the behaviors we take.

In our early years, we start to build confidence and self-esteem, which is heavily influenced by the interactions we have with our parents. A youngster needs to feel loved by those who are close to him or her and have a strong belief in their own skills in order to be healthy. This enables kids to face new obstacles with courage and deal with hurt, disillusionment, and annoyance.

It should come as no surprise that kids who have great self-esteem also grow up to be successful, happy people who can rely on themselves and get good grades. Not because they are inherently smarter than their classmates but rather because they absorb intelligence and have the capacity to grow and get better over time.

Depending on the child's developmental stage, the degree of self-esteem varies slightly, but it's crucial to be able to spot the warning indications of a lack of confidence in the child's skills. This could be the outcome of uncontrollable outside factors or bad things your child has gone through. Children with poor self-esteem, for whatever reason, often "encourage" others to try new things because they lack confidence in their own talents. This is due to their frequent dread of making mistakes and their aversion to taking on new tasks out of a sense of inadequacy.

Confident and resilient individuals, as well as to maximize their chances of developing these traits in them.

Gaining a deeper understanding of how words and actions affect children's emotions is the first step. That's precisely what this book was meant to assist you with. The most prevalent "parental trap"—excessive praise and rewards—is demonstrated, along with practical ways to prevent it. These include helping kids build their self-esteem and confidence so they can grow up to be happy, successful adults.

How to Get Over Poor Self-Confidence

Decide on your ideal self and follow your truth: The different identities that people give you are what depresses them most of the time. These are frequently negative representations of the person you would want to think you are. Start separating yourself from the labels that have been placed on you by family, friends, and other acquaintances if you have been living up to them. Give no one the authority to define who you are. This is your life, and you were made specially for it. Nobody is able to completely comprehend your potential and ability. Begin distancing yourself from whatever it is that others wish you to be. People often tell you who you ought to be in order to satisfy their wants and for their benefit. Rather, wisdom is thinking ahead to the person you will be proud to be and planning your life around that vision. This distances you from the quest for other people's validation and instead concentrates on making your validation sufficient for you, which makes you an incredibly confident individual.

Anticipate being unaffected by what others think of you: Being preoccupied with the idea of being flawless in the sight of others turns you into a slave to those whose praise you seek. I've seen time and time again that people are avaricious. There's no assurance that someone will genuinely value and recognize the amount of work you put in to show them who you are. You can liberate yourself from the negativity of others and the constraints they attempt to place on you when you begin to treat other people's opinions as unimportant. When someone is incapable of doing anything, they frequently assume that others would likewise fail at it in order to relieve some of their own self-doubt. So, learn to give your thoughts about yourself more attention. Yes, that is your real business.

Embrace a supportive network that is progressive and upbeat: The majority of the people in your life have an impact on your attitudes, behaviors, beliefs, and ideas. Spend time with people who love and care about you, surround yourself with new experiences, establish new friendships, find a personal mentor, and strengthen your bonds with them. They will turn into the comforting voice of encouragement you need to bolster your confidence during your moments of uncertainty. Assemble a circle of people around you who are wiser and more experienced than you are. This network of support will serve as a stabilizing force and aid in your gradual development.

Develop a winning mindset: When your attitude is unchecked and unevaluated, it can easily turn negative. Your perspective on life, other people, and yourself will determine how far you can go. When things get hard, do you give up and complain right away? You become a lifelong victim of circumstances as a result of this. Decide that you are going to approach every day of your life with a winning attitude and optimism. Your attitude draws people and opportunities to you. A nasty person is the last person anyone wants to be around. Making the decision to act positively may not come easily at first, but success is achievable. Your attitude will be more consistent if you let your decisions guide your life rather than your emotions. It's challenging to be in a positive mood when you follow your emotions. Have a positive attitude at all times, and let that choice serve as your benchmark. When your emotions are unstable, this serves as your shield.

Establish challenging and ambitious goals: Put your goals in writing and make sure you can see them every day. Invest some time in classifying your plans so that you can assess your performance more easily and work at your peak efficiency. Your objectives might be established in accordance with your personal priorities. The most time and effort should go into achieving your top priorities. Your days become more productive and confident after you get up each day, knowing exactly what has to be done to reach your goals. To make sure you have the time and chances to accumulate success, you must create goals. Your confidence will increase in proportion to the amount of goals you accomplish. Your life will go in the path of your dreams when you have goals in mind. When you find yourself falling short of specific objectives, ask for help from others. Being self-sufficient is not the definition of confidence; rather, confidence is the ability to trust people and let them assist you in reaching your goals.

One of the biggest enemies of productive dialogue is sarcasm. It can be harmful whether applied by you or when it's being used against you by others. We chose the word "against" because it serves as a kind of protection. It's a cheap joke that hides animosity and insecurity, and it usually indicates depression of some kind. You won't benefit from it in the long run as an attitude, and most people will view you as a jerk. There are two ways to deal with sarcasm: either you ignore it, or you engage in a wit-war with the person. A third choice would be to confront them directly about their sarcasm, showing them that it is a non-constructive attitude that adds nothing to the discussion. Say something simple like, "Sarcasm?" Really? Is that the best you can do?

Ignoring sarcasm transfers the power from the caustic individual to you. You can act as though you didn't hear what they had to say, or you can respond in a way that clearly echoes their sarcasm and lets them know you don't care for meaningless babble. You can always try to explain your points and defend your position, but the majority of sarcastic individuals are not interested in hearing you out. If they were, they would listen to you instead of coming up with a clever retort to put in your face. You should give the facts if they make sense, but if you aren't speaking with a character that is well-adjusted, try not to waste your time or energy trying to make an impractical argument.

Personal insults and threats won't get you very far, he said. An aggressive individual is not someone who exudes confidence. You put your own reputation at risk when you try to damage someone else's reputation by talking behind their back or spreading untruths about them. You don't need anything more to motivate you to pursue your work if you possess a strong personality, charm, abilities, and professional qualities. Furthermore, it is common knowledge that the individual who initiates or disseminates the rumor is concealing something personal from which they are attempting to deflect attention. They wouldn't go through all that trouble if that weren't the case.

Using the phrase "always and never" to characterize someone's demeanor or attitude in a conversation is a surefire method to encourage them to avoid you. It is never appropriate to say things like, "You never listen to me, you're always late, you leave me hanging, or you never call." These stereotypes will cast you in the role of a victim, and you should never be perceived that way by others. Use phrases that are more strategic, such as "you've been late a lot lately. What's going on in your life?" Alternate: I saw you nod off during our conversation; is everything alright? In this manner, you can truly ask them to explain why they are running late or aren't paying attention rather than making them feel your annoyance.

Most of the time, emotional vampires can drain your self-confidence. Make an effort to stay away from them. Even though they make an effort to remain hidden under a façade of friendliness and interest in your life, you will be able to identify them quickly. They will either not listen at all or only listen long enough to interject and tell you their story. They will never be curious about what you have to say and will spend most of your time together talking about themselves. They will try to stop you and hold you back by saying things like I can never imagine you play the cello - after you say you enrolled for cello lessons, or: who would've thought you'd get this far - when you got a promotion; or: you have to tell me how you managed to pull off these jeans with that shirt - when you are dressed perfectly normal. Your ideas, plans, goals, and achievements will never be measured realistically. Their goal is to exhaust you to the point where you are unable to speak highly of yourself. As soon as you schedule your meeting and hang up the phone, you will experience emotional weariness. Seldom will they provide you with a meeting time and date right away. They'll make an effort to appear important, and they need to find time in their schedules to be with you. Your time with them will seem to last twice as long as it does. And you will immediately allow yourself some time to heal after you do eventually part ways before giving them another call.

These individuals are proliferating like rabbits, and you shouldn't allow them to diminish your authority. Dealing with them directly is the best course of action, not in an antagonistic, violent way, but in a kind way. They will taste their own medicine if you can employ the same strategy, but it's usually preferable to walk the higher road. The right thing to do is to turn away from them. Naturally, not in the middle of your date, but rather methodically and gradually. Try meeting with them in groups if you are unable to completely avoid them. You can tackle them down because you are two against one, and they won't be the center of attention, even if they try. Minimize your interactions with them and make an effort to decline their calls or attempts to schedule a meeting every other time. These subliminal cues will eventually instruct them to emotionally and physically keep their distance.

You should give them a helping hand if you can't let them go since you love and care about them. With their attitude, emotional vampires typically cry for assistance. Therefore, if you can work through some of their issues together, be a sincere friend and lend a sympathetic ear. that knows? Perhaps now is the right moment to make amends for being the vampire that stole someone else's joy at one point in your life.

Talk Clearly

You are aware that, among other verbal cues, speaking loudly is an indication of trust. Being noisy disturbs other people's minds. This is the same as forcing people to walk around you by getting in their way. It suddenly makes it logical to relate the volume you're discussing to your religious beliefs. The speech "Secrets to Success" by Eric Thomas is the ideal illustration of this. You can view it by visiting the website or YouTube account. These are the things that great conversationalists and seasoned speakers like Eric have to teach you about speaking up in public.

It provides them with Existence: When you become too loud, it's your turn to talk. Everybody is focusing.

Trust: When you speak clearly, any feelings of anxiety or dread go away. People are conditioned to feel this way and are unable to resist it. Why? You wouldn't express things so plainly if you didn't believe what you were saying.

Passion: It goes without saying that your voice will grow louder and more rapid if you are passionate about the topic. The question arises when you become quiet once more out of nervousness or concern that your voice may reach a new pitch. Keep them from doing it. Be astute. Keep quiet. Show off your enthusiasm. That is something that the public values.

Is it necessary to make noise all the time? No. No. In your debate, is it appropriate to speak at or somewhat above everyone else's volume? It's obvious that you may feel irritable. And perhaps you are, but that's not because of your length; rather, it's a personality trait. You need to make an impression, stick out from the crowd, and confidently deliver solutions. In most cases, being silent doesn't encourage you to do that.

It is not distracting to make the proposal loudly, ask for feedback thereafter, sit calmly, and keep others around you in mind. Just because someone doesn't articulate himself clearly doesn't mean that it should be annoying to prevent the discourse from shifting away from their point of view. Being present and enthusiastic when narrating your experience is most definitely not distracting.

Grin, idiot

Anxiety and anger make us do a lot of foolish things that we are unaware of. One that is particularly harmful but is not mentioned enough is when we join a conversation with a completely blank expression on our faces. You should be aware that your face will appear expressionless and uninviting, regardless of your level of anxiety or unfamiliarity.

You didn't cross your arms because someone told you not to. However, the same impulse that keeps our breasts and stomachs safe from predators also keeps our faces clean from anything even slightly amiable or welcoming.

The way that all of us aspire to achieve that charming, carefree, yet intelligent expression on our faces is this:

Make your own forced facial expression first. In general, go right immediately, grinning broadly. In the same way as saying "Hey! What kind of day did you have?

Pick a word that will be quiet for the first several minutes. Depending on who you ask, you don't have to smile all the time like a crazy person since that's not how you feel. Even though you're not laughing while you're by yourself, you're content when you're contemplative or serene.

After that, genuinely maintain a loose face. Try to maintain a relaxed expression and express whatever emotion is on your face rather than worrying about whether or not to smile all the time. Not just the oral muscles but also the muscles in your pupils. At this stage of the conversation, all you need to do is make sure you're not confronted with stoniness because anxiety kind of locks things up. Watch out for casual conversations—no one is ever happy all the time.

It simply takes a few minutes to start paying attention to facial expressions, which is crucial. Spend time and money putting the above rules into practice at least a few times. You'll revert to your previous habits precisely as you did when you were anxious as long as you are aware that they are important.

Advice For Talking With Anyone About Anything

When a stranger is meant to strike up a conversation with us, we all detest the awkward stillness that ensues. Maybe you're sitting next to a new colleague at a company gathering. It could be that you run into a friend of a friend during a reception. How far along were the initial introductions? What happens, though, when you're up against stiff competition in a high-stakes scenario like a job interview? The blind date remains in place after that. If you want to, how do you make it the start of anything significant?

That has a specific conversational style. If your personality is extroverted, you should be able to carry on a conversation or at least place yourself in any social setting without too much discomfort. If, however, you are an introvert, these situations will make you shudder. The only thing on your mind is how badly you want to run. While many people fall somewhere in the middle of the introversion-extroversion spectrum, everyone experiences periods of extreme success and moments of complete failure just before something spectacular happens.

Success in the small chat is similar to performance in other social environments, such as job interviews, social networking, and Internet conversations. The fundamental idea is that you may establish common ground with those you speak with by exhibiting the appropriate levels of patience, sensitivity, and self-disclosure. I believe that the person-centered therapy approach developed by Carl Rogers may be the most useful manual for small discussion circles. Rogers made important advances in clinical psychology and therapy during the 1970s by instructing therapists on how to better listen to their patients, communicate their feelings, and transform their thoughts into ideas that promote healing. Needless to say, you will not be conducting psychotherapy sessions in your conversations with strangers. However, you may use Rogers' observations to help you get over the awkward moments in your conversations with strangers. When you combine these nuggets of wisdom with a bit of social science, you have a powerful formula for success regardless of who you are conversing with or how much you detest or avoid social situations.

Pay attention

Too often, when we're meeting someone new, we attempt to pass the time by spreading rumors about ourselves. It's probably best to speak after you've listened. Of course, someone will start the conversation, but talks will flow more easily if you and your partner actually listen to each other and don't plan your next move.

Employ reflective empathy

Restating what you have heard, or at least what you think you have heard, is the next communication phase. It will show that you've been paying attention and invite your discussion partner to clarify if what you've learned differs from what you truly believe to be true.

Activate your nonverbal cues.

Rogers was renowned for his ability to read the body language of his customers. It works best if you focus on how you believe the other person is feeling based on their nonverbal cues rather than how you are feeling on the inside. Change the subject if you perceive that they are not happy with the direction the conversation is taking. Some people prefer to keep things light when talking about sex, politics, and religion. Acquire the skill of interpreting nonverbal cues like as attitude, eye contact, and hand movements to gauge the effect of your actions.

Avert rash decisions.

You will be less likely to misinterpret the person you are speaking with if you adhere to the previous three steps; yet, we are all prone to drawing judgments about people based on scant information. When they first meet, things are not as they seem. You are less likely to base a judgment incorrectly on outside cues if you have paid close attention, replicated what you have heard, and maintained an open nonverbal channel.

Acquiring The Ability To Receive Praise

It's quite simple to reject encouraging remarks from others when you struggle with self-esteem because you don't think they apply to you and believe you don't deserve them. The issue lies in the fact that you deserve those compliments. Say "thank you" and accept the praise gracefully if someone tells you that you look great. If you react negatively and let your pride get in the way, people will stop complimenting you.

Praise must not originate solely from other individuals. You lose sight of the significance of praises to yourself if you are constantly seeking acceptance from others. When you get dressed up to go out, gaze in the mirror and tell yourself that you look amazing. Congratulate yourself on your effective scenario management. By gazing at yourself in the mirror and appreciating the good things in life, you might learn to complement yourself. Your praises serve as confirmations. You shed any uncertainty and use language that doesn't cast doubt on your abilities. Rather, they validate your abilities. Rephrase your thoughts, and when you catch yourself thinking negatively, let go of them and come up with a fresh way of putting them. Sayings such as "I am not good enough" are an example of how you truly become inadequate. It is self-destructive, so stop it. Reframe negative thoughts with affirmations of your own worth, and if you catch yourself thinking about them, rapidly replace them with positive thoughts.

While out with friends one day, I seem to recall receiving praise for an item of clothing I had chosen. We were in a store and went by a mirror, but I wasn't used to people praising me. My friend told me I looked nice, and I looked in the mirror at the same moment and realized I looked better than I was giving myself credit for. The difficulty is that your problems with self-esteem get worse the more you criticize yourself. A child will grow hopeless if you tell him he is hopeless every day of his life because he will believe what is said so frequently. Similarly, you may become a much happier person by regularly showering yourself with compliments.

You are worth it, and when you start using praise on yourself as well, you restore your value and feel much more confident about who you are, which is something you should enjoy. Trust me, it works. Begin modestly by praising little things in yourself as you glance in the mirror every morning. When you start giving yourself more credit and bringing more optimism into your life, you also start to think differently and understand that you have the same right to that happiness as everyone else.

Making compliments

You are aware of the moments when someone says something to you that makes you feel good but have you ever considered how others feel when you give them a compliment? It's known as paying it forward; learn to return the favor by praising someone else for every kindness that you receive. How much benefit is that to you? Assisting them with whatever troubles they may be having with their self-esteem. It's well worth the practice because it boosts your confidence and improves the feelings of others.

In addition, while you are occupied with praising someone, your mind is diverted from pessimism; when you begin to positively impact your life and take stock of it, confidence blossoms. You may feel good about yourself through your own activities rather than depending on other people to do it for you, and that's a great weapon to employ against feelings of insecurity and low confidence. It also empowers you with self-worth and dignity and demonstrates that you don't always need to rely on other people to validate who you are—your own deeds speak volumes about that.

By offering compliments, you not only make someone else's day a little better—people around you can also lack confidence—but you also add something positive to yourself. It helps you feel less dependent on other people's approval and more whole. Telling someone they've done well never hurts, and if you make today about looking outside rather than within, you'll discover that there are a lot of people out there who are looking for acceptance, and you can help them by just being kind. You also gain an understanding of your own abilities, which is crucial when trying to build self-confidence.

Eliminate all bad ideas.

Avoid having self-doubt by asking yourself, "Can I do it?"

Simply swap out the words and believe that you can succeed instead. Observe the distinction.

So, eradicate fear and self-doubt. Have no fear of anything. The thing that ties us and our thoughts together and causes obstacles in life is fear. So get rid of your nervousness and believe that "I can accomplish anything I set out to do." Remind yourself of this. Place it somewhere you'll see it frequently. Use it as your computer's screen saver.

Eliminate anxiety

Anxiety is more than just mental. It assaults your thoughts first, then moves on to your body, causing panic symptoms like rapid breathing, tense muscles, and occasionally even lightheadedness. It interprets an idea as an actual threat and makes your body ready for "fight or flight." Opting out of the aforementioned symptoms is the greatest method to fend this off. Do a placid and tranquil demeanor while slowing down and deepening your breathing. This can help you quickly overcome your panic attack because your mind is unable to be both calm and worried at the same time! You can fight these attacks with meditation, and you will eventually overcome them. In the process, you will also acquire a great deal of self-confidence. Studies have shown that in order to achieve happiness and calmness, meditation engages the left and right brains in different ways. It's the brain vitamin par excellence!

The fundamental nature of your character is defined by the way you view the world. You may be experiencing persistent uneasiness and anxieties if you have a natural internal resistance to repeating daily affirmations. However, if you find that repeating daily affirmations comes easily and with joy, that suggests that you have positive traits in you. Self-help methods like meditation and daily affirmations can assist you in breaking bad thought patterns and behaviors. Start by determining the causes, origins, and other details of your concerns. Meditation is the most effective method for reducing stress, anxiety, and phobias.

Recognize your advantages.

You cannot distinguish fantasy from reality with your intellect. You may, therefore, conjure up anything that will relieve your stress by using your imagination. Your mind will accept everything you can dream up, so feel free to let your imagination run wild. Your mind will believe this story if you imagine yourself cocooned into a white cloud, floating in the blue sky, and having a great time.

In any circumstance where you feel like you are losing all ability to deal and you are unable to recall any technique, meditation, or daily affirmation, just separate yourself from your body, become light, and levitate above it. View the world and yourself objectively from above. This will put you at ease right away. When that personal sense is absent, neither are the emotions, and you will be at ease with the circumstances as you watch yourself as a third party from above.

Regularly visualize the positive thoughts:

A concept comes to life through visualization. When you use positive and uplifting thoughts to create a mental movie of your future, it manifests itself miraculously! You can experiment with this method to see the incredible outcomes. You might have a meditative or trancelike state of mind while doing this.

Try using both positive and negative language and see the difference:

Try experimenting with different words and seeing how they affect your life to have a better understanding of this wonderful technique of positive thinking, often known as daily affirmations. Consider the impact of beginning your day with a positive assertion. Likewise, if you're brave enough, try experimenting with some negative ideas to see if you can notice a change!

Say, "It's a beautiful day," as an example.

I am able to accomplish my goals.

I'm doing well.

Think instead, "I can't do it."

It won't take place.

Do you notice the difference?

Advice on how to unwind

To ease your tension and anxiety, try one of the various meditation techniques, daily affirmations, or guided meditations. There are also additional immediate methods for managing your anxiety. Below are explanations for a few of them:

Breathing By paying attention to your breathing, you can safely refocus your mind away from your concerns. By deliberately slowing down your breathing, you can naturally de-stress and release tension.

What precisely is Rebirth?

The word "rebirth," which literally translates to "rebirth" in English, describes an inner growth and transformation method that delves into one's mind in order to release oneself from emotional constraints and ingrained thought patterns. Deeply ingrained in Eastern philosophy, the idea of Rebirth is frequently connected to the never-ending cycle of life, death, and Rebirth.

The Reasons Behind Rebirth Although the practice of Rebirth has roots in many different philosophical and spiritual traditions, Buddhism and Hinduism have had a significant influence. The idea of "Samsara," or the never-ending cycle of birth, death, and Rebirth, is fundamental to Buddhism. Buddhism seeks "Enlightenment" or "Nirvana" as a means of emancipating the self from the constraints of this material cycle.

The idea of reincarnation—in which the soul cycles between life and death in order to progress spiritually—is ingrained in Hinduism. The concept of evolution and growth via numerous incarnations or worldly lifetimes is connected to Rebirth.

A Contemporary Perspective on Rebirth
Rebirth has found application in more contemporary settings, including psychology, therapy, and mindfulness exercises, in addition to its spiritual foundations. According to these readings, Rebirth is frequently seen as a way to break away from emotionally draining experiences, constricting thought patterns, and prior traumas. Through a variety of methods, including guided meditation, deep breathing, and emotional inquiry, people attempt to

confront and heal the hidden aspects of their minds.

The objective of contemporary Rebirth is a process of inner development and personal growth that helps people get past emotional challenges and enhances their quality of life. While rebirth techniques vary greatly, they frequently combine profound meditation, emotion exploration, and breath exercises to support mental and emotional health.

In the end, Rebirth is a practice that offers a way for inner Rebirth and personal development while embracing old spiritual traditions and adjusting to the demands and difficulties of modernity.

Both the ancient and modern conceptions of Rebirth place a strong emphasis on the pursuit of personal growth and the development of a deeper knowledge of both oneself and the outside world. It is thought that one might liberate oneself from ingrained anxieties, traumas, and conditionings that impede one's ability to advance personally by working on the depths of one's unconscious.

In conclusion, Rebirth offers a chance to delve into one's innermost thoughts, motivated by spiritual traditions' ideas of life, death, and Rebirth. The idea of Rebirth, despite its ancient origins, is still applicable and flexible in the present day, when it is seen as a tool for personal fulfillment, emotional healing, and inner development.

The respiratory technique

A deep and deliberate breathing technique called "RebirthingBreathwork," or just "Rebirthing," aims to release built-up tensions in the body and mind, fostering emotional healing and personal development. This method is influenced by Eastern philosophy, namely the ideas of "Prana" (life energy) and the life-death-rebirth cycle.

Rebirthing _ Breathwork is taking a series of deep, even breaths while concentrating on breathing without pausing in between breaths. By inducing a condition of controlled hyperventilation, this breathing technique raises the body's oxygenation level and helps people let go of mental and physical strain.

It is typically advised to practice in a continuous, fluid rhythm, with no breaks in between breaths. It is normal to feel tingling, warmth, strong feelings,

RebirthingBreathwork is widely regarded as a successful technique for resolving emotional blocks, tensions that have built up, and prior traumas. Repressed feelings or traumas that may have lain unconscious can arise as a result of the practice. It is safe to face and let go of these feelings.

In order to promote calmness and well-being, deep, controlled breathing can assist in lowering stress and tension levels in the body. People can achieve substantial personal growth and increased self-awareness via the process of healing and releasing. Rebirthing facilitates the transformation of constrictive mental patterns, fostering an optimistic and expansive outlook. Enhanced vitality and energy levels might result from more oxygenation of the body. Some claim to have had bodily benefits, including improved blood flow and relaxed muscles.

Maintain the Beat. Sustain your breathing at a steady, smooth pace. Avoid holding your breath or hesitating in between breaths. This consistent Beat will facilitate the development of a controlled hyperventilation condition.

Monitoring Emotions: Start observing the sensations in your body and mind while you practice. There could be sensations of lightness, warmth, or tingling. Accept your emotions without passing judgment and give them permission to surface as needed.

Expression of Emotions: You may feel strong emotions during RebirthingBreathwork. It's critical to let these feelings surface and express themselves. It's okay to cry, laugh, or scream during practice. Allow feelings to surface naturally.

Unwinding: Following a period of deep breathing, gently slow down your breathing and resume your regular, peaceful breathing. You can unwind and process the event at this point.

Observation: After doing the RebirthingBreathwork, give the experience some thought. You can process what you've been going through by keeping a journal or talking to a friend or reputable therapist about your feelings.

Recurrence If desired, RebirthingBreathwork can be used on a regular basis to alleviate emotional tensions or further blockages. New insights and liberations may arise from each session.

Expert Oversight It is best to practice under the guidance of a therapist skilled with this approach if you are new to rebirthing or are attempting to address deep trauma. A professional can help you with any strong emotions and carefully lead you through the process.

RebirthingBreathwork is a discipline; therefore, keep in mind that it calls for self-care and respect. Practice in a secure setting, and never push your body or emotions. Rebirthing can eventually aid in your personal development.

Establishing And Reaching Goals

Setting goals and attaining them are essential steps on the path to developing the proper mindset, success, and happiness. Objectives offer guidance, inspiration, and a feeling of direction. These are the benchmarks that indicate our advancement and guide us in the direction of our goals. This chapter will cover methods and approaches for creating goals that are realistic, maintaining motivation, monitoring development, and acknowledging accomplishments.

Having Specific Objectives

Setting goals that work is the cornerstone of success and a happy outlook. Goals that are precise and well-defined offer concentration, direction, and a feeling of purpose. Here's how to make your aims clear:

1. Establish Your Vision: To start, decide what success and happiness look like for you. For you, what does success mean? Which areas of your life would you like to strengthen or improve? Your vision is the compass that directs the creation of your goals.

2. Establish Particular Goals: Particular goals are precise and well-defined. Rather than aiming for something general like "getting in shape," make your objective more focused, like "running a half marathon in six months."

Setting specific goals enables you to clarify your objectives.

3. Make Measurable Objectives: Measurable objectives let you monitor your development. Decide on metrics by which to judge your progress. If your objective is to read more, for instance, establish a quantifiable goal like "read one book per month."

4. Establish Achievable Goals: Objectives ought to be difficult but reachable. When you set goals, take into account your current resources and capabilities. Unattainable objectives can cause dissatisfaction and demotivation.

5. Relevant Goals: Make sure your objectives align with your overarching

vision and core principles. They ought to be personally significant and in line with your goals.

6. Time-Bound Objectives: Establish a deadline for reaching your objectives. Setting a deadline makes things feel more urgent and keeps you on course. Think about the phrase "Save $5,000 for a vacation in one year."

7. Divide Up Bigger Objectives: If you have important long-term objectives, divide them up into smaller, more doable tasks. These more manageable objectives allow you a sense of success as you progress.

8. Put Your Goals in Writing: Committing to your goals in writing helps you stay

motivated. To stay focused, make a list of your objectives and refer to it frequently.

9. Visualise Your Success: One effective strategy is visualization. See yourself accomplishing your objectives. You can improve your drive and attitude by visualizing success.

Maintaining Motivation

The motivation behind achieving goals is what keeps us going. It strengthens your will and helps you stay on the path even in the face of difficulties. This is how to maintain motivation:

1. Link Goals to Values: Recognise how your objectives relate to your basic

beliefs and ambitions. You are more likely to maintain motivation when your objectives are consistent with your values.

2. Find Your "Why": Look closely to identify the fundamental causes of your objectives. What positive effects will these goals have on your life? Your "why" acts as a strong incentive.

3. Establish Rewards: Decide on prizes for completing tasks or accomplishing particular objectives. Rewarding behavior generates anticipation and positive reinforcement.

4. Break Down Goals: As previously indicated, divide more ambitious objectives into more manageable steps.

Recognizing and appreciating these incremental successes might help increase motivation.

5. Remain Responsible: Discuss your objectives with a mentor or close friend who you can rely on to hold you responsible. It can be encouraging to know that someone is keeping tabs on your development.

6. Visualise Success: Consistently picture yourself accomplishing your objectives. Experience the feelings that come with achievement. Visualization has been shown to increase confidence and motivation.

7. Remain Inspired: Surround yourself with motivational people. Go through

books, watch videos, or make connections with people who have accomplished comparable things. Their tales have the power to inspire you.

8. Overcome Difficulties: Be ready for and anticipate difficulties. Consider obstacles as chances to show your resiliency and dedication to your objectives.

9. Make a Vision Board: A vision board is a picture that symbolizes your objectives. It might have pictures, sayings, and symbols that serve as a reminder of your goals.

10. Develop self-compassion: Treat yourself with kindness as you travel. It's normal to experience failures and

periods of low motivation. Recognize your accomplishments and cultivate self-compassion.

Leaving when things get difficult

By all means, leave a poisonous relationship as soon as possible, but before you do, give yourself some space to consider whether or not your actions are motivated by your fears. Did you really put forth the effort to give your all at work, or was quitting more convenient than dealing with a cruel supervisor or obnoxious coworkers? If you are insecure about your skills and performance, you may succumb to pressure too quickly or avoid confrontations or disputes. I know it is simpler to curl up in a ball, but that is not a sustainable way to live. We may overcome obstacles and emerge from them stronger, happier, and more prepared to face the next one.

Delaying

For those of you who are feeling overwhelmed and struggling with self-doubt, this is a pretty frequent strategy. The truth is that waiting until the last minute to do something is nearly always a surefire way to fail. But you are aware of that already, aren't you? Avoidance is when you have to study for a crucial meeting but choose to spend that time organizing your pants closet or binge-watching Netflix instead. Even if you may convince yourself that you'll do it later, your true statement is probably "I can't cope." I doubt I'll be able to make it. You don't succeed as a result since your focus is diverted from the task at hand.

Dating the incorrect man

Why do you go on dates with individuals you know aren't compatible with you? It's not surprising if your relationship ends soon if you're not like slobbering, beer-guzzling people who enjoy lounging about all day. Maybe you stay in a long-term relationship despite your dissatisfaction because you are scared of what will happen to you if you leave. You know that all of this is undermining your efforts to be happy, but you persist because you don't think you deserve any better.

These are some of the common elements that appear in self-destructive behavior, and at this point, it's a good idea to ask yourself, "What am I afraid of?" The mind can jot down this question and consider the first thought that comes to mind.

Let's take a closer look at the reasons behind your self-perception and assume that you worry that you will never make a decent mother. Did you experience anything that led you to believe that? Did you have any prior experience that influenced your views on becoming a mother and raising kids? How was your upbringing? Did you have a good upbringing, or did you feel unloved or ignored? Are you concerned that it will change your way of life or lead to conflict with your partner or family? Do you think you're too young or too old, or are you unsure of your ability to adapt? All of these problems are solvable, but you have to face them head-on.

Face the fear you are experiencing head-on by laying it out and addressing it. We merely think there are monsters under the bed until we look and realize it's nothing but our anxieties. Monsters under the bed don't actually exist.

The counterfeit You

I must bring up something that has been all the rage lately: imposter syndrome. In essence, this is the feeling that you are not as competent as people perceive you to be. Yes, you are a fake, and you have no business being where you are. This applies to your abilities, social standing, employment, and pretty much everything else. Surprisingly, the phrase was originally used to characterize accomplished women who believed that just because they were women, they didn't deserve such a high rank. This now applies to anyone who believes they are lying to people because they secretly believe they are undeserving.

If you doubt yourself, find it difficult to evaluate your own abilities, or attribute your achievement to uncontrollable circumstances like good fortune, you might be experiencing impostor syndrome. You can even strive to overachieve and create unachievable goals for yourself, or you might try to minimize your accomplishments. All of this may result in a worrying loop where you are unable to internalize your accomplishments and never give yourself credit for anything.

According to a recent independent study conducted in 2019 by Access Commercial Finance, among the 3000 persons surveyed in the UK, more women (66%) than men (56%) reported experiencing imposter syndrome at some point in the previous year. Even while more and more women are launching their own firms and moving up the corporate ladder, it appears that many of them are anxious about their peers realizing there isn't a Wizard of Oz and feel like imposters. It's possible that women encounter it more frequently because they were raised in a culture that still finds it difficult to accept them as being on par with males in terms of skills.

Many women still believe that they "Don't have a head for business" or "Got where they are today because of their looks," despite the overwhelming evidence to the contrary. Long-term exposure to it exacerbates the issue because it increases your risk of developing chronic illnesses linked to stress and keeps you from appreciating your accomplishments.

I have some useful suggestions that will enable you to reconsider your actions that are causing harm to yourself. Make a mental note of anything that strikes you as particularly accurate as you go through each one. It all comes down to altering ingrained behaviors and mindsets, so be patient and ease into each one rather than expecting results right away. You will gradually experience the advantages.

Give up, think small.

Though it limits your potential, you might wish to occupy as little space as possible in the globe. What would happen if you had a clear goal in life, something you were passionate about and felt driven to achieve?

You can achieve anything if you think large, and when you do, the possibilities are endless. Make a list of your goals, interests, and aspirations while sitting down. Then, include your abilities, attributes, and skills. You have the freedom to pursue your goals in life, and only your narrow-mindedness will stand in your way.

Handling the Unavoidable Failures: Pardon Yourself

Since we are all fallible human beings, errors, mistakes, and setbacks are inevitable. It's crucial that you forgive yourself, endure them, and utilize them as motivation rather than allowing them to sap your motivation.

Since forgiveness is such a strong weapon, be sure to forgive yourself as well! When someone truly forgives you, don't you feel happy? Naturally, of course! Thus, treat oneself with kindness. Make the most of the situation and consider any failure or mistake as a lesson that will make you smarter.

Since prevention is preferable to treatment, make an effort to foresee obstacles and setbacks. Examine your prior failures and the reasons behind them. Was there anything about your objective that wasn't founded on a deep comprehension of what matters most to you? Were you motivated by a negative self-image or a hopeful vision of who you could be, or were your reasons for taking on this task out of alignment with who you actually are? Have you attempted to solve the problem as a whole, as opposed to segmenting it into smaller, more doable pieces? Recite your affirmations aloud and complete the practice where you focused on imagining the qualities about yourself that you find most appealing. Reread your progress and your list of minor victories and accomplishments from your diary and success calendar to keep yourself motivated. Recall that Rome wasn't created in a day.

Shortcuts are adored by all. They typically require less work and help us get where we want to be faster. Furthermore, there are tricks or shortcuts you can employ with willpower.

Boost Your Mental Capacity

Recall that willpower is like a muscle that can be built and enhanced with the right kind of workout. Thus, try doing the exact opposite of what you usually do once in a while! Every time you make a routine adjustment, your self-control improves. Try using your non-dominant hand to unlock doors or clean your teeth, for instance. It will compel your brain to create new neural connections linked to learning and innovative thought processes. After you've completed little milestones like these, try advancing to more important objectives. To gain self-control, just do the opposite of what you usually do.

Play with Your Mind

To overcome an initially impossible goal, take a mental shortcut and convince your mind that the task at hand is more of a habit shift than a difficulty. Make it a regular part of your day if your objective is to start something new, learn something new, or change something. It will feel awkward and foreign at first, but eventually, it will become automatic and part of your routine. If you are attempting to learn a language, for instance, consider eating breakfast while listening to a foreign-language radio program; if you are trying to launch a business, schedule regular time in your calendar for one-on-one meetings with a mentor; if you want to strengthen a significant relationship in your life, set aside that regular time for private one-on-one time with that person. Avoid dwelling too much on the specifics. Simply incorporate it into your daily routine.

Maintain High Glucose Levels!

Every time we try to do something, whether it's going above and beyond to complete a task or overcoming an obstacle, we use the limited glucose energy that our bodies have. Our brains and muscles receive their energy from glucose. Our willpower reserves decrease along with our blood glucose levels. Therefore, consume regular meals that are high in protein and carbohydrates, such as a sandwich made with lean meat and cheese between two slices of whole wheat bread, to keep your energy supply (and consequently your willpower) topped off. Additionally, never begin a task when you're hungry!

Letting Go and Becoming Forgiven

Why is it so difficult to let go of your deeply ingrained self-beliefs? Why is it so hard to think that you're capable of changing? Regularity and consistency are the most significant drivers. You've been hearing the same things about yourself in your thoughts for so long that you've begun to believe them. By thinking back on earlier remarks you've made about yourself, you can even get yourself ensnared in your negative self-talk. How is it possible? Why is it that you can recall events from so many years ago with clarity, yet you have to pause and consider your lunch three days ago?

You see, the secret is in the repetition. The truth is, you've never truly been able to let go of your old, negative self-talk. Rather, you've given it a safe haven in the recesses of your thoughts, and it knows precisely when to come out, stick its ugly head out, and attack.

While the tidy freaks clean their homes every day or at least frequently, even the dirtiest and laziest among us occasionally do so. You desire neat surroundings with room for you to flourish, so you hoover your floors, clean your linens and clean the glass. All of us, though, frequently neglect to dust and polish the mirrors within our own heads. You may give yourself permission to harbor self-criticism and pessimistic ideas and make bad choices for years at a time, sometimes to the point where they are nearly impossible to eradicate. Healthy self-esteem is encouraged by a clear mind, free of the mistakes we've made in the past.

You see the ghost of the past when you're afraid. It shows up when you're angry, scared, or isolated. It follows you when you are unable to conquer an obstacle; it passes by like an old friend you would prefer not to see. However, even when you've had the bravery and resolve to command it to leave, it keeps coming back to reinforce all the negative self-perceptions you have. It's difficult to let go of decisions you made a long time ago because of this ghost of your past.

You have to forgive yourself before you can have a healthy sense of self-worth. You need to put some effort into getting rid of your inner critic. Just concentrate on the portion of your mind that recognizes your inherent goodness.

Activity: Experiences with Self-Esteem

Use the box below to complete this task. List five situations that, whether positively or badly, have impacted your sense of self-worth. Jot down any thoughts you had while having the experience, any afterthoughts that persisted, and your feelings as you went. Though it may seem overwhelming, don't panic. As you work on this, maintain composure and be honest and mindful.

You Have the Power To Change The World.

"To be the person you could have been, it's never too late." — William Shakespeare.

Since discovering and pursuing your mission in life is the most important thing you will ever do, love comes second to your objective. Purpose is the foundation of success. Discovering your mission gives you a connection to something more powerful and thought-provoking than yourself.

Doves are beautiful creatures. They have been employed for generations to convey messages to kings, generals, and other important people due to their extraordinary abilities.

The Dove in society serves the powerful even if it has little.

A lot of people were content to settle for second best. The misfortune of civilization is the power of the norm. You have the capacity to be greater and fulfill your goals. The world has lost, choked out, buried, and suppressed human potential. Your purpose is one thing that improves everything.

But there's one very important distinction. Pursuing your objective is not a methodical undertaking. Moreover, it is impossible to plan for every aspect of this process in advance. It's a riddle. It's an investigative process. It's also a journey; as you start to feel the stirring of your mission pushing you forth in life, it's as if an undiscovered part of yourself is beckoning you. In the words of Dr. Myles Munroe, "Man is like an onion." One layer at a time, his potential is revealed until everyone is aware of who he is.

You are being called to become even more of an adult, to take ownership of how you use your power, and to have even more faith in your Creator. However, you have to make the decision that nothing less than the achievement of your ambition will do.

But you have to be open to accepting and believing that God has a purpose for your life.

One of the most significant mental shifts you may have to make is to think that once you begin living out your mission, serving others, and solving problems, you will be taken care of.

If you just prioritize the needs of others and develop a passion for fixing a problem you see in the world,

You will be taken care of after that.

The greatest leap of faith that your purpose is asking you to take is to surrender your neurotic need to survive and place your survival in the hands of your Creator.

And for YOU to keep your unwavering attention on how you may help other people.

To put it simply, if you make it your job to take care of God's children, He will take care of you. Stated differently, life supports that which life supports.

You knew the true nature of reality from the moment of your birth. Perhaps you were at a loss for what to say.

Perhaps you were unsure about the precise words to use. However, a part of you understood that you would easily survive if you lived out your purpose and put others' needs first.

This does not absolve you of the need to exercise caution, judgment, and strategy.

However, what I'm trying to convey is that if you put your attention on helping others, you can be sure that all of your needs will be met.

Additionally, keep in mind... You, too, are a child of God. Thus, remember to take care of yourself as well as God's children as you focus on them.

You know you are coming close to your objective when your plans for the next phase of your life start to make no sense. When you are requested to carry out a task for which you are unfamiliar and uncertain about how to proceed.

Why do you think your current skill set is inadequate for the task you have been called to?

Caroline Myss offers the perfect answer.

She says we are being drawn into unknown land since this trail is free of any traces of the past.

In other words, you can serve without having to commit to a significant amount of healing along the road you are called to. You are able to go to work right away.

The more emotional baggage you carry, the longer it will take you to start moving ahead.

Therefore, have faith in your dreams, recognize that you are being called to a magnificent new purpose, and make every effort to quiet your mind and let go of your anxieties. And focus on taking small, bold action steps each day.

Trust your instincts and let go of your fear. That's the goal, instead of allowing your anxiousness to be suppressed and heeding your gut.

God does not call forth the strong. Everyone follows, but God does qualify those who are called. And it includes YOU as well.

YOU are being invited to live your mission, rise above your existing state of existence, and have a positive impact on the world.

Making this leap can assist you in taking care of your loved ones, reaching your goals, and enjoying abundance.

Giving up your fear of surviving and dedicating all of your efforts to compassionately resolving the world's problems is the price. You are untouchable, and no one from that location can harm you.

Develop the ability to speak up for what you want and need.

Never hold back from communicating your demands and desires, and always do so in an assertive manner. Make sure that everyone around you understands and respects your boundaries. It supports the preservation of confidence, mutual understanding, and self-respect.

Allocate time for interests that bring you a sense of fulfillment.

You can feel accomplished by engaging in some pastimes like painting, cooking, gardening, playing an instrument, or creating something artistic. Happiness and confidence are raised by this.

When things are difficult, remind yourself of your former achievements.

Remember the difficult times you have experienced in the past and how you overcame them to reach some worthwhile goals. This will instill the mindset of "I CAN" in you, which will inspire you and bolster your self-confidence.

Seek out novel encounters to broaden your perspective.

Try new things: try new things like traveling to new locations, getting to know new people, taking up new hobbies, and learning about other cultures. These are all effective strategies to develop your personality and advance your personal development. You can have a clear path towards your goals, increase your confidence, and extend your perspective by taking on new challenges and experiences.

Utilise constructive imagery to envision your perfect self.

Give yourself some time to engage in self-visualization. Close your eyes and see your accomplishments and characteristics. Your confidence and motivation will both increase with this constructive self-imaging.

Put your happiness first.

Prioritize your happiness over any sense of selfishness because doing so can contribute to your general well-being. If you are content, you can make other people happy, which will increase your confidence, give you a sense of accomplishment, and satisfy you.

Make use of creative channels to communicate your ideas and emotions.

Writing, drawing, or experimenting with new cuisine are examples of creative pursuits that can assist you in expressing your ideas and feelings and improving your mood. Without worrying about being rejected, share your artistic endeavors with those in your immediate vicinity.

Embrace a positive quotation and affirmation culture.

Post inspirational sayings and affirmations on wall posters in areas you frequent, such as your office, the door to your bathroom, and the mirror in the room where you spend most of your time. You are reminded of your skills, resilience, and strength by these affirmations.

Accept accountability for your decisions and actions.

Recognize that the decisions and choices you make are your responsibility and that you are accountable for the results. It fosters personal development, increases trust, and gives you decision-making authority.

Hold fast to your morals even in the face of difficulty.

Always uphold your principles in the face of difficulties and outside pressure, even if you are tempted to compromise them. Remaining true to your principles improves your integrity, feeling of purpose, and respect for yourself.

Develop a sense of humor.

A sense of humor is a highly useful tool for better stress management and for navigating the ups and downs of life. Laugh often and look for humor in everything. When you can, laugh out loud, watch comedic films, and read jokes.

The Empirical Evidence For Self-Compassion

Self-compassion science is grounded in various psychological theories and paradigms. Among the most well-known is the self-compassion theory created by psychologist Dr. Kristin Neff. Three primary elements comprise self-compassion, according to her theory: self-kindness, common humanity, and mindfulness.

Self-Control

When faced with challenging circumstances or setbacks, practicing self-kindness entails treating oneself with compassion and understanding as opposed to severely criticizing or passing judgment on oneself. It entails giving oneself kindness and compassion, accepting one's flaws and limitations, forgiving oneself, and partaking in self-care practices that advance wellbeing and wellbeing.

People can develop a stronger feeling of self-compassion and wellbeing, as well as increased resilience and self-efficacy to better handle challenging circumstances by engaging in self-kindness practices.

Collective Humanity

Acknowledging that errors, suffering, and defects are all a part of the human experience is what is meant to be understood by the concept of common humanity or connectivity. These experiences are common to everyone at some point in their lives. This entails admitting that obstacles are a common occurrence for everyone and that they are a necessary aspect of life.

Seeing our suffering or challenges as particular, unrelatable, or humiliating can lead to emotions of isolation and loneliness, which can be lessened by acknowledging our shared humanity. Rather, acknowledging that others have experienced comparable circumstances can foster a feeling of unity and common humanity.

Realizing that everyone has difficulties can help people to understand and care for others more. This supports the development of a stronger sense of well-being, well-being, and social connectedness.

Being mindful

Being mindful entails giving your entire attention to the present moment, judgment-free. This encompasses your emotions, ideas, and physical experiences. To do this, one must completely inhabit the current moment as opposed to ruminating on the past or fretting about the future.

Developing a non-judgmental awareness of one's experiences is another aspect of mindfulness. It involves letting go of the need to control or avoid your feelings and experiences and instead allowing yourself to go through them. Rather, you accept them as an inherent aspect of being human.

Because mindfulness trains people to become more aware of their own thoughts, feelings, and experiences, it can help people become more self-aware. This can greatly aid in improving your understanding of your own wants and desires, which is beneficial for fostering self-compassion and self-esteem. Additionally, it supports you in making more deliberate and thoughtful decisions in your life, which has a big positive impact on your self-control.

The Advantages of Self-Care

- Better mental health: Studies have linked self-compassion to a decrease in stress, anxiety, and depressive symptoms, as well as an improvement in emotional resilience and psychological wellbeing [18][19][20].

Enhanced physical wellbeing: Research has connected self-compassion to enhanced physical wellbeing, including enhanced immunological response, decreased blood pressure, and less inflammation [21]. It even reduces the chance of diseases like cardiovascular disease that are brought on by stress [22].

● Higher self-esteem: People with self-compassionate attitudes towards themselves tend to think better of themselves, and this is correlated with higher levels of self-esteem.

Better handling of setbacks: Since self-compassion offers consolation and support through trying times, it can also assist people in handling obstacles and setbacks more skillfully.

● Increased drive and personal development: Unlike what the general public thinks, self-compassion is not connected to laziness or self-gratification. Rather, studies have indicated that self-compassionate people are more driven to better themselves and accomplish their objectives because they are not constrained by self-blame and self-criticism.

In general, improving their general wellbeing and quality of life.

Someone once said, "Your identity is not what holds you back. It's who you think you're not at all." Making sure your beliefs are motivating, uplifting, and supportive of you is a crucial step in learning how to develop self-esteem.

I'm assuming you are aware of this basic truth: "High self-esteem is the path to achievement." Strong self-esteem is always necessary, regardless of your connections, occupation, public activities, account, or anything else. Then, how would we cultivate self-worth?

What if we treated it as a problem?

1. Describe the problem.

2. Think about it.

3- Examine the resolution.

4- Assemble the answer. Easy! (Well, I know it's not that easy, but let's approach it that way.)

Describe the issue: At its core, self-esteem usually consists of drawing distinctions between oneself and other people. Collectively, we purposefully or unconsciously group people; we value and respect certain individuals, ignore or treat others patronizingly (odious but true); it's all about how we perceive ourselves in relation to one another; we logically assign ourselves a trait that helps us stay in the public eye. When you don't think well of yourself, you start to think that everyone else is better than you.

This is based on the nub of the problem, which is that you have a false self-perception. Why is this a false viewpoint? This is because you are too self-basic and have created a false incentive for yourself when comparing yourself to other people.

2. Give it some thought - Let's start by using a parallel. Feeling low about yourself is similar to putting an inflated price ticket on an item in a storefront. Assume that the items in the shop were you and your coworkers. Despite the fact that you all produce or do very identical work and are paid fairly, the shop owner has given them a $100 sticker price while only giving you a $1 one. This is obviously wrong on his part. And consider who is responsible for placing an improper value ticket in an item at a store—that's right, you are since you are the one who manages your own life. In

light of this, you are the one who can handle it; you may increase or develop your self-esteem, for example, by placing the right sticker price on it.

Second, self-esteem isn't something that comes naturally to you; you frequently see sisters and brothers who have rather distinct personalities. It's a topic that many people can relate to. Fortunately, learning how to raise or develop one's self-esteem is possible. Interesting fact: according to surveys, almost 60% of us struggle with poor self-esteem. In this regard, you are undoubtedly not alone.

3. Examine the solutions. To understand how to increase self-esteem, you must examine yourself in order to gain an

accurate target viewpoint on who you are. As a collective, we possess both strengths and weaknesses; note them so that, upon recognition, we can build upon our foundation. What do you excel at? What activities do you enjoy? What would you like to excel at? What seriously do you do? What activities do you dislike?

Next, describe what's most important to you. Refrain from taking praises from people of the other sex or your boss too seriously. It could feel better, but it won't last. Focus on the bigger picture. Most of us want a happy and fulfilling life; we want to realize our potential and surpass it; we want to accomplish things; we want to think like this.

Everyone is unique these days, but if you want to improve your sense of self-worth, you have to admit that you need to change. Nothing special will occur unless you do.

Here's a comprehensive summary: Examine it, add to it if necessary, choose the ones that pertain to you, be honest, and look over your list of strengths and weaknesses to see how they stack up.

Respect for Oneself: Quit beating yourself up and stop analyzing yourself.

Attitude: While bad things do happen, they usually revolve around the problem rather than the remedy. Any setback should be viewed as a learning opportunity rather than an accident.

Relationships: Mix with people who are positive, not negative.

Social aptitudes: Make an effort to be calm, courteous, kind, and well-mannered. Respect, pay attention to, and understand the needs of others.

Examine your own inclinations.

Accept change; don't be pessimistic or afraid of it.

4. Give, collaborate, and share. Establish the solution: Pay close attention to developing the aforementioned

aptitudes. Be resolved in your perspective; this is usually important.

Imagine yourself succeeding in your endeavors, interacting with others, or meeting someone with the right attributes. Representation is a fantastic tool that people in elite sports routinely use, so it will help you feel more confident and develop self-worth.

You will find that you become more successful at your job, in social situations, and when you go out with someone if you can learn how to increase your self-esteem. If your self-esteem is low, it might feel like a downward spiral that makes you feel hopeless and prevents you from doing anything, so instead of giving up, stay determined.

Effects On Personality And Social Bonds

1. Eroded Self-Esteem: Codependents frequently struggle with low self-worth and feelings of inadequacy. This could start a vicious cycle of looking for outside affirmation and acceptance to cover this emotional gap.

2. Unhealthy Relationship Dynamics: Conflict, inequality, and frequently reciprocal codependency are traits of codependent partnerships. Instability, conflict, and ongoing stress can result from these processes.

3. Difficulty in Determining and Maintaining Healthy Boundaries: When someone's rights and personal space are

repeatedly violated, it can lead to a sense of annoyance and bitterness.

4. Emotional Tiredness: Taking care of other people's needs and problems all the time can be emotionally taxing. Burnout, overwhelm, and exhaustion are common experiences for codependents.

5. Health Implications: Codependency's stress and emotional upheaval can have negative effects on one's physical health, such as anxiety, insomnia, and even physical illnesses.

6. Social Isolation: Because their primary emphasis is on their codependent relationship, codependents may distance themselves from other friends and family members.

8. Maintaining Unhealthy Patterns: Codependency, which frequently stems from learned behaviors and family dynamics, can be passed down from generation to generation in the absence of intervention.

It is essential to comprehend the consequences of codependency in order to inspire people to get help and take the required actions in order to break free from these harmful habits. We'll go into greater detail on the underlying causes of codependency, self-evaluation tools, and doable recovery techniques in later sections of this book, providing a clear route to better relationships and self-care. In order to overcome codependenttendencies and promote healthy relationships, we will examine the root reasons for codependency, the value of self-awareness, and techniques for reestablishing self-esteem in the ensuing chapters.

Practical Step: Starting a Journal of Self-Love

As a useful tool for fostering self-worth and self-love, consider starting a self-love notebook. Write down your accomplishments, positive affirmations, self-care experiences, and times when you showed compassion for yourself in this diary. Think back on experiences that represent self-worth and self-love, and acknowledge your achievements.

This journal will become a record of your journey towards stronger self-worth over time.

In the following chapters of this book, we will explore practical methods for breaking codependent habits, creating and maintaining strong personal boundaries, and valuing self-care. A crucial first step in this process is rebuilding your self-esteem,

As we discussed in Chapter 2, intuition is a theoretical idea. Once you grasp its concept, there is no way to analyze it other than to express it as you feel it. It combines your spiritual, physical, and cognitive aspects, enabling you to process your experiences, feelings, ideas, and physical sensations. It guides you towards what is best for you and takes your interests into account. It explains how to interact with society.

Since intuition is an immediate view of reality, it is unaffected by the application of logic. Consider it as an immediate fear of something you are seeing or experiencing. It's an intense human experience that defies explanation.

As we've mentioned previously, when you confront a friend about something, there's a little voice in your head that tells you they're not speaking the truth. Before your intellect can tell you what to do, your body is responding. For example, express gratitude to your body for its intuitive processes that rescue you from danger. Though the concepts you have acquired are stored in your mind, in some instances, your body provides you with real sense data that you can rely on more than your thinking.

If someone can learn to be conscious of their dreams, they can take control of them, as demonstrated by the lucid dreaming example in Chapter 2. It implies that even when you're asleep, it's possible to distinguish between reality and dreams. However, the majority of people do not possess this ability, and that is perfectly acceptable.

But this simply goes to demonstrate that you can think creatively in regular life if you can imagine unreal events while you sleep. The body, on the other hand, just reacts; it does not "think."

You have no influence over what transpires with the body. This is how the truth is drawn. You can tell that body language is honest because it simply responds to the information that is given to it. The cognitive filter process does not exist. This is why observing nonverbal cues, body language, and gestures—especially unconscious ones—may teach us so much about nonverbal communication. As we've shown, the body doesn't lie—unless, of course, you're a skilled actor or actress lying on purpose, in which case, your body does not lie.

Even while acting solely on the basis of your intuition might not always be sensible or advantageous for the circumstance, you might attempt to determine whether what your intuition is telling you about a person—for example, a colleague—is genuine. For example, you sense from your gut that this colleague is not focusing on the task at hand, but instead of confronting them, you consider how best to approach them. Many people, for various reasons, ignore their intuition as they go through life. Growing up in a family that discourages emotional expression, whether done so in a healthy way or not, is one factor. This is how a lot of young individuals who had harsh parenting grow up, thinking that showing their feelings makes them appear weak. Rather than embracing their emotions, they learn to repress them out of fear of rejection or criticism. As a result, kids don't develop their intuition or confidence as they get older. This can be fixed by fostering an atmosphere that encourages healthy emotional expression, which will increase self-assurance and faith in one's intuition.

All people have feelings, regardless of what those sentiments may be. Individuals who experience poor self-esteem as children must overcome this in order to trust their gut feeling and act responsibly in their surroundings. The use of exposure treatment is one strategy to address this. As we've already discussed, the basic tenet of exposure therapy is to do something that makes you uncomfortable. Over time, you will be able to train yourself to accept an action or scenario more and more when you subject yourself to it for an extended length of time when it causes you anxiety or discomfort. As you get more adept at "taking the heat," you will start to develop stronger coping mechanisms and how to tolerate its "negative" impacts. Put yourself in those scenarios gradually to increase your tolerance and a good reaction to the previously "embarrassing" situation if you lack confidence, especially in certain settings. Put another way, push yourself outside your comfort zone.

The secret to developing faith in your intuition is to have a level of self-confidence that enables you to take specific actions. Being self-assured entails learning how to handle obstacles and pursuing goals that will improve your life circumstances. It could take some time for you to accomplish certain things as you develop and enhance your confidence. That's alright, but you have to approach it gently and gradually in case you make mistakes along the road.

Enhanced self-assurance allows you to place greater faith in your instincts in any given circumstance. But as we have already shown, intuition cannot be measured, nor can it be evaluated to determine whether it is accurate at the time it occurs. Recall that this is what your intuition tells you; it is what is in your spirit.

Emotional Intelligence

In the last chapter, we touched on emotional intelligence and how employers value it highly. The terms "emotional intelligence" and "emotional intelligence" were coined by scholars Peter Salavoy and John Mayer. The current definition of emotional intelligence is the capacity to identify, comprehend, and regulate one's own emotions. It can also mean being able to identify, comprehend, and manage other people's feelings. To put it simply, emotional intelligence (EI) is the capacity to recognize that human behaviors are influenced by emotions, which can also affect other people. You can have a good influence on both yourself and other people by developing emotional self-management skills.

The foundation of emotional intelligence consists of these five elements:

● Self-awareness: Possessing self-awareness enables one to recognize one's advantages and disadvantages and appropriate responses to others and situations.

● Self-regulation: People with high emotional intelligence (EI) who possess self-awareness can control their emotions and rein them in when necessary.

- **Motivation:** People with high EI typically possess greater motivation, which leads to greater optimism and resilience in the face of adversity.

- **Empathy:** People who are compassionate and empathic interact with people more successfully.

The general population finds emotional intelligence to be a very appealing notion, notwithstanding the criticism. In some industries, this subject is even more popular. Employers are increasingly using personality tests throughout the hiring process to find candidates with higher emotional intelligence (EI), as this suggests they will be better team players or leaders.

Why Emotional Intelligence Is Important

Over time, emotional intelligence has become more and more significant, particularly in the workplace. Not every emotion you were experiencing that day has to be suppressed just because you enter your place of employment. Though most individuals tend to think otherwise, emotions are always present on the job and are typically controlled to maintain professionalism. Individuals frequently act as though they are emotionless when at work in order to prevent coming across as unprofessional.

Because working cultures have changed, emotional intelligence has become increasingly crucial in today's society. The majority of work done these days is done in teams rather than alone. Forward-thinking companies understand that addressing emotions at work improves the atmosphere for employees. This would imply that individuals need to be more sensitive to both their own and other people's sentiments. Better emotional intelligence makes a person more flexible, which is a necessary trait in today's fast-paced world.

More emotionally intelligent leaders tend to have happier teams, which reduces significant expenses like turnover and boosts overall productivity. As we previously covered, those with higher emotional intelligence typically have happier lives outside of the workplace.

A person can enhance their emotional intelligence in the following ways:

● Consider your feelings: A person starts to become more conscious of themselves as they think back on their feelings. To begin developing emotional intelligence, consider your own emotions and your response to unfavorable circumstances. You can start to regulate and control your emotions when you are more conscious of which ones you are experiencing.

● Seek an alternative viewpoint: Everybody has a unique perspective on the world. Begin by seeking input from others and make an effort to comprehend your personality in emotionally charged circumstances.

● Observe: Attempt to gain a deeper comprehension of your actions when you have begun to become more self-aware. Start noticing and paying attention to your feelings.

● Take a little break: Before acting, take a minute to consider your feelings. In highly charged settings, this could be challenging to accomplish, but with experience, it will become second nature.

● Increase empathy by learning the "why" behind someone else's feelings or emotions. Put yourself in their position and try to imagine what it would be like to be them.

●

Opted to take advice from criticism: criticism is unavoidable in life, even though nobody enjoys hearing it. Make the choice to absorb criticism rather than immediately going into defensive mode to raise your emotional intelligence.

Practice: It has been demonstrated that emotional intelligence may be enhanced with some practice, but it does not happen instantly.

11) Inspiration

A factor that contributes to success is motivation. Our unwavering motivation is the force that propels us to take necessary action. Discovering the motivation to learn success is just as crucial as actually doing it. We could accomplish it in the real world once we have clarified it in our imaginations.

While motivation is important, it is not the only factor in success. In isolation, motivation lacks the other corroborating elements that comprise the entire picture. That being said, while having the motivation to act is already quite an achievement, it is not yet complete.

12) Determination and Commitment

A goal's pursuit is not solely motivated. While motivation plays a significant role in the process of a goal, it cannot function on its own. The same level of devotion and drive must be shown towards it.

In order to achieve the success we desire, we must dedicate ourselves to achieving our objectives, being determined throughout the process, and possessing the drive to see our projects through to completion. Whether it's success in the workplace, in business, or in education, a blend of these three elements is always required.

13) Lastly, Be Content With What We Do: If we discover joy in our work, excellence is possible. Having fun while doing something is the greatest way to do it. As we pursue our goals, we enjoy and take pleasure in whatever it is that we are doing. Only then will we be able to achieve excellence and feel fulfillment in our work.

The greatest individuals in history were never made to do anything against their will. They performed it out of love for what they do. They possessed commitment, determination, enthusiasm, and self-motivation. We could also use this for ourselves.

Everything begins with us, and we begin with the drive to reach our goals. We then pursue our objective with a fierce desire, a determination to proceed, and a commitment to succeeding in life. Not the money or our carer, but rather the enjoyment we felt from start to finish, is what matters most of all. Enjoy ourself!

Thinking Positively

Positive Thinking: What Is It?

It is imperative to acknowledge that adopting a positive mindset does not entail acquiescing to every scenario or acting as though there are none at all. It doesn't mean you have to come up with a plan for how you're going to keep running from reality or from experiencing these issues within. It doesn't mean you have to live a wholly innocent life, refusing to believe that anything bad could ever happen or that you have to accept things as they are.

Thinking positively enables you to pause and acknowledge that life can be unpleasant at times. It enables you to recognize when something is not working well or when changes are necessary. The problem with positive thinking is that it takes a constructive rather than an adversarial attitude to these circumstances. You will stop and look for the most productive ways to start thinking about the environment around you rather than trying to avoid or keep making things worse.

You normally begin thinking positively when you speak to yourself. It is the inner monologue you have on repeat all the time, telling you what to think, how to think, and why you should keep thinking the way you do. It centers on the notion that you will speak to yourself in a manner consistent with your own mentality. Negative people frequently talk negatively to themselves, while positive ones tend to have a positive outlook and style of thinking. They will convince themselves that they are incapable of succeeding or of doing anything successfully, and with time, they usually come to believe it.

Most of the time, self-talk and monologues are a result of experience; your perception of the world is shaped by your past encounters, which makes it difficult for you to engage with people in social situations. If you already have a propensity for negativity, it is a serious issue. Reflecting on how you interact with yourself allows you to frequently trace that behavior directly back to a previous experience. Maybe you felt that you never had any true friends who genuinely liked you, or maybe your parents never thought well of you. It's possible that you felt this way for other reasons. Still, the inner monologue you create will undoubtedly influence how you engage with the outside world.

When you think in such a pessimistic way, you tend to fall into a mindset that is difficult to escape. Over time, your negativity will only make you feel worse. But the opposite is also true: thinking positively will make you feel like you can actually keep thinking positively and will also attract more positive things into your life. Instead of feeling stuck or like you've made a mistake, you'll find opportunities to keep moving forward.

www.ingramcontent.com/pod-product-compliance
Lightning Source LLC
Chambersburg PA
CBHW052141110526
44591CB00012B/1811